The Read Aloud Cloud

An Innocent's Guide to the Tech Inside

Forrest Brazeal

WILEY

Copyright © 2021 by John Wiley & Sons, Inc., Indianapolis, Indiana

Published simultaneously in Canada

ISBN: 978-1-119-67762-8

ISBN: 978-1-119-67764-2 (ebk)

ISBN: 978-1-119-67765-9 (ebk)

Manufactured in the United States of America

For general information on our other products and services please contact our Customer Care Department within the United States at (877) 762-2974, outside the United States at (317) 572-3993 or fax (317) 572-4002.

Wiley publishes in a variety of print and electronic formats and by print-on-demand. Some material included with standard print versions of this book may not be included in e-books or in print-on-demand. If this book refers to media such as a CD or DVD that is not included in the version you purchased, you may download this material at booksupport.wiley.com. For more information about Wiley products, visit www.wiley.com.

Library of Congress Control Number: 2020939431

SKY10023225_121120

For the cloud folks.

About the Author

Through a decade in the tech industry, Forrest Brazeal has installed software updates during a live cataract surgery, designed robots that perform machine learning on pizza, and kept his sense of humor the whole time—even while rapping about serverless technology in front of hundreds of developers.

Now a senior manager at A Cloud Guru, Forrest has been named one of Jefferson Frank's top seven global AWS experts. In 2018, Amazon Web Services recognized his community work by naming him one of the original AWS Serverless Heroes.

His webcomics about life in the cloud reach hundreds of thousands of readers and have been cut out, tacked up, reshared, and PowerPointed at workplaces from Google to Disney. He also speaks at public and private events around the world on the business and technology of cloud computing. *The Read Aloud Cloud* is his first book.

Forrest has a master's degree in computer science from Georgia Tech and a postgraduate certificate in nonsense from wherever Dr. Seuss did his doctorate. He lives near Charlotte, North Carolina, with his wife, two children, and an unmanageable collection of old books.

Acknowledgments

There comes a dark point in the development of any book, but particularly one so bizarre as this, when you become convinced that you have jumped the rails and created something that nobody in their right mind would ever want to read. This is where it helps to have deadlines pushing your shapeless hunk of nonsense back on track. So: thank you, deadlines.

The entire team at Wiley embraced the challenge of publishing whatever this book is, but none more so than Devon Lewis. Devon immediately "got" this strange project and championed it from the very beginning, providing a tireless flow of ideas and support all the way through the production process.

My employers at Trek10 and A Cloud Guru warmly encouraged me while I was writing. I, in turn, warmly encourage you to patronize Trek10 and A Cloud Guru.

My friend, mentor, and colleague Drew Firment never let his enthusiasm for this book flag, even when I did. Thanks, buddy.

My technical reviewers—Jared Short, Corey Quinn, and Ken Winner—willingly exposed themselves to early, unstable doses of this book, for which we can all be grateful. Any misrepresentation of the cloud that remains is mine alone.

The deranged Roomba on page 3 is probably Ben Kehoe's fault.

Many of the prehistoric computers in Chapter 2 were drawn from "live models" at Seattle's marvelous Living Computer Museum. My thanks to the AWS Hero program, and particularly the indefatigable Rebecca Marshburn, for making that cross-country field trip possible.

Emily, Kenneth, and Joanna tolerated this project longer than any reasonable humans should. Thank you for everything. I promise I'm done now.

Foreword

Cloud computing and related shifts such as serverless are major changes running through the tech industry. As with all such major changes, this comes with opportunities (often involving the gnashing of teeth and pulling out of hair), challenges (the gnashing of hair and pulling out of teeth), and—if we're very lucky—humor. In the past, tectonic shifts in technology—from the office PC to the smartphone—have brought us stalwarts such as Scott Adams (Dilbert), Randall Munroe (xkcd), and GapingVoid. I am delighted that our industry continues its tradition of poking insightful fun at itself with the addition of Forrest Brazeal to that pantheon.

In the cloud, serverless, and DevOps world, there has been no one more insightful and "incite-ful" than Forrest. Cutting through the trees to see the wood, Forrest's wit has become a guiding light. His cartoons have not only delighted but meaningfully questioned our approaches—all good humor is based on truth—from the tribal nature of DevOps to the building of Towers of Babel such as OpenStack. The skill and technological knowledge required to understand a technological change, to pinpoint its failing, and to devastate an entire edifice of marketing and a bastion of management consultants with a single cartoon should not be underestimated. It also requires an element of bravery to poke the massive capitalist bear with a stick of truth. Forrest has that skill, he has that bravery, and he frequently uses it. We praise him.

And praise is the right word. I am delighted and honored to call Forrest a friend, but more than this, his work has helped transform an industry, putting it on an even keel. In this world of billion-dollar acquisitions of small tech startups, we technologists can often get carried away with ourselves. The ability to create a virtual world quickly translates to a belief that we can solve world hunger through the excellence of our minds and the alteration of a few digits in a line of code. Such delusions regularly need to be brought back down to Earth and our own hubris and fallacies bared naked for all to see. This is a service that Forrest provides. I cannot tell you how many times I have laughed, cried, and held my head in my hands muttering "oh my God" at one of Forrest's cartoons.

It is that art of using humor to hold up a mirror to our own ego, our runaway beliefs, our inflated self-confidence, and the ability to ask that one question that sets Forrest apart. Technology, as with many other industries, often breaks down into collectives, into warring tribes, each convinced of our own rightness as we face each other down across the blinding light of our blazing production environments. Forrest simply shows us how comical the situation is, how comical we are, and how a different perspective is possible. And so, with no more egging of the pudding and no further ado, it is my pleasure to introduce you to the delightful world and work of Forrest Brazeal.

—Simon Wardley

Researcher, Leading Edge Forum.

Chapter 1
WHAT IS "THE CLOUD"?

I've looked at clouds from both sides now,
From up and down, and still somehow
It's cloud illusions I recall...
I really don't know clouds at all.

—JONI MITCHELL

So the cloud...is my data, like, up in the sky, or what?
Ha, ha, ha! Pass me that bag of chips.

—YOUR UNCLE MIKE

What is the cloud?
Is it here or there?
Should it be allowed?
Should you even care?

Your hotel key,
your boarding pass,
The card you swipe to pay for gas,

Your doorbell,
toothbrush,
thermostat,
The vacuum that
attacked your cat,

They all connect the cloud and you.
Maybe they shouldn't, but they do.

5

Now, each day brings new tales of hacks
—the data leaks, the bot attacks—
Or buggy apps that will not load.
And, helpless, you lurch down the road.

"It's in the cloud." (You wave your hands.)
"That thing that no one understands."
Because you've learned to raise your guard:
The cloud is weird, remote, and hard.

But this is not a scary story.
Unfamiliar territory
Though the cloud may be right now,
Don't you ever wonder:

HOW?

How did we get from
where we've *been*—
Books on paper, ink
in pen—
To this cloudy future where
we *are*?
Is there maybe a chance
we've gone too far?
How does it work, should it
be allowed,
And WHAT IN THE WORLD
IS THE DOGGONE CLOUD?

You'll hear from smug
unhelpful tutors:
The cloud is just someone else's
computers.
Since, by a process of osmosis,
You already kind of
know this,

Let's be real: it's also more.
A whole lot more, behind this door.

So turn the page,
and let's explore.

What Is "THE CLOUD"?

Well, as you've noticed by now, this is a different kind of book about the cloud.

I've been building cloud applications for quite a few years, and I still have trouble explaining to my friends and family exactly what it is I do. In fact, a couple of years ago I realized that I had just kind of given up.

Sample conversation:

A NORMAL PERSON: "So what do you do for work?"

ME: "Gargle, gargle."

This is not because the cloud is so complex and mysterious. Doctors and scientists don't have trouble saying, "I'm a doctor or a scientist," and their jobs are a lot harder and stranger than mine. I think I just got into my own head.

But I also know I'm not alone. There's a whole industry full of smart and accomplished cloud professionals gargling their way through the dinner parties they totally get invited to, because they never learned the tools to explain what they do. Their fancy computer science degrees taught them to balance binary search trees and negotiate the Border Gateway Protocol but not how to say "I write programs that run on someone else's computers."

And really, the larger problem is abstraction. It can be hard to explain the building blocks of the cloud because the concepts don't *relate* to anything in the physical world. We all have some intuitive understanding of why a doctor exists. What exactly does a "cloud architect" build, and why does it matter?

The best way I can think of to explain is to draw a bunch of cartoons.

So I made this book for techie people like me to give to their non-techie friends. Or their children. Or their CEOs. Or just to keep on their desks. No shame in that.

10

I've tried to write from the perspective of someone who is new to the idea of "the cloud," beyond a vague understanding that your iPhone stores its pictures there. I hope that by the last page, you will have not only a better understanding of the ways in which cloud affects you as an ordinary consumer but also a broad grasp of how cloud systems are designed, built, and maintained—you know, the work that my colleagues and I are so congenitally unable to explain.

(Side note: Do you know how hard it is to write hundreds of rhymes about the cloud? Of course you don't; you're much too smart to try that. I'm regretting it already, so please be kind.)

These little "Word to the Nerd" sections at the end of each chapter are totally optional. I'll do my best to keep them interesting, but they're mainly here for context and to make this book look slightly less like the product of sugar-fueled madness that it is. You can get all the important stuff just from the rhymes and pictures. And I hope you will.

See, the thing is, I love the cloud. I want everyone else to see it the way I do: As a Rube Goldberg machine made out of millions of tiny tubes. As the survivor of decades of cutthroat evolution, red in Bluetooth and claw. As a magic show, a Dr. Seuss fable, or sometimes even a gothic horror story or a bank heist.

I want the cloud to take its place where it belongs: in your imagination, as filled with wonder and possibility as any field of endeavor mankind has yet created.

Shall we begin?

Chapter 2
EVOLUTION OF THE CLOUD: A PREHISTORY

Extinction is the rule. Survival is the exception.

—CARL SAGAN

The cloud is just mainframes all over again.

—YOUR GRANDPA WHO HAS A PENSION FROM IBM

In the beginning, when the world was new, If you needed a computer, then your options were few.

The MAINFRAMES ruled.
They were heavy and slow.
Their lights made a wicked
and predatory glow.

They were HUGE,
they were HOT,
they made HORRIBLE ROARS,
And they trailed a tail of
cables all over the floors.

They were also EXPENSIVE. Like, epochally so. Only schools and corporations could afford one, you know. So the users had to share it on a TIMESHARE PLAN. They took turns submitting programs on their PUNCH CARDS. Man, you might wait there for hours with your punch cards and such.
It was better than nothing, but not by much.

WHY SO BIG? A COMPUTER HAS MANY CRITICAL SYSTEMS

CPU

RAM

LONG-TERM STORAGE

INPUT

OUTPUT

POWER SUPPLY

PERIPHERAL DEVICES

BUT THEN...something happened. Computers EVOLVED.
The cost and size problems began to be solved.
Punch cards were out like a vestigial fin.
Microscopic integrated circuits were IN!

A new kind of beast waddled out of the murk:
The desktop computer was ready for work.

advances in microprocessor technologies_

pdp-10
[1966]

xerox alto
[1973]

missing links

vector 1
[1977]

apple macintosh
[1984]

mainframes
large, expensive, hungry

⟩ PCs
small, cheap, tasty

A PERSONAL COMPUTER?
Wasn't that nice, though?
You could work from your desk, from the beach, from an ice floe.
No punch cards, no sharing,
no waiting in line.
And if something still had to be centralized? Fine!
Because central computers, too, shrank to the max.
We labeled them SERVERS and stacked them in racks
In a SERVER ROOM, where they'd be happy and free,
Maintained by the creatures who work in IT.

21

You'd think we'd be done here. What more could we need?
Computers were small now. They ran at great speed.
But here was the problem, the minuscule pain:

ROOMFULS OF SERVERS ARE HARD TO MAINTAIN.

The people who fix them take ages to train,
And every small business began to complain.

22

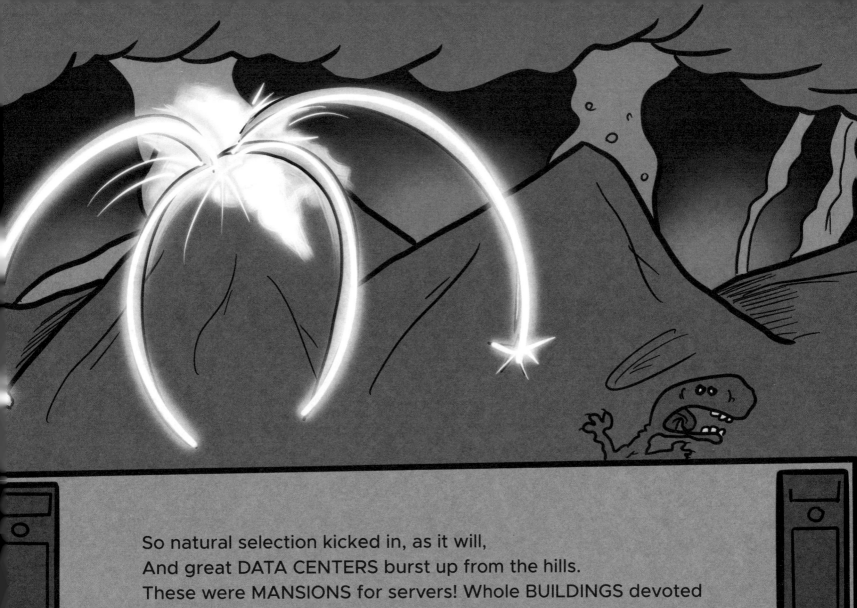

So natural selection kicked in, as it will,
And great DATA CENTERS burst up from the hills.
These were MANSIONS for servers! Whole BUILDINGS devoted
To central computing! The market exploded!

No one knows who first thought it, who said it aloud,
But these clusters of servers, majestic and proud,
Began to be known, in a word, as the CLOUD.

But that's just half the story.
The cloud is no good
If you can't connect to it
from your neighborhood.
For the cloud to get LOUD,
we need something more yet:
Connections. Pipes.
Plumbing. A web. Or...a net.
And the biggest dang net
you can possibly get
Is that great innovation:
THE INTERNET.

Evolution of the Cloud: A Prehistory

The cloud is the natural convergence of two of the biggest technological innovations of the last half century: cheap, compact computer hardware on the one hand and the Internet on the other. (We'll look more closely at the Internet in the next chapter.)

And yet, some people will still tell you that the cloud is hardly a patch on the original version of centralized, networked computing: the mainframe.

Mainframes: The OG Cloud

Anybody who worked in an office in the 1970s and 1980s has some sort of mainframe story. Giant, cabinet-sized computers. Programs fed in via punched cards and run in batches. Time-sharing: groups of people waiting their turn to access the shared resources. Special cooling systems because of the phenomenal energy required to run all that hardware.

The thing is, though, the mainframe had some right to be enormous because it could do *everything*. It had storage, CPU, and networking, all onboard. Within the range of its capabilities, it was fast as all heck. And individual mainframes were frequently customized further, with all kinds of hardware and software foofaraws that made them a perfect fit for a particular business. You could think of a mainframe computer like a very big, very warm, very expensive pet dinosaur that belonged only to you and could get you wherever you needed to go.

Mainframes are absolutely still in use today—in fact, studies estimate that as much as 70 percent of *production workloads* (computer programs that do important work) still run on mainframes. Our core financial infrastructure, our airlines, our utilities...all to some extent rely on hardware and software designs that are 30 to 50 years old.

Mainframes have downsides. They're unwieldy, expensive, and getting harder and harder to keep in running order as the generation of engineers who specialized in them reaches retirement age. But mainframes got one essential thing right: they centralized the hard work of running shared software, like databases, so that regular users could focus on getting their jobs done. And any improvement on the mainframe would have to check that box.

PCs: The Hardware Gets Smaller

The trend away from mainframes began in the early 1980s when manufacturers like IBM and Apple began mass-producing "desktop computers" small enough to run from home. No longer was computing something that happened only while plugged into a behemoth machine at the office. And so for a number of years, desktop applications like Microsoft Office helped decentralize work, pushing more processing responsibilities onto client computers.

These PCs still needed to connect to central systems for some work tasks, though. And as hardware advances continued to drive down the price and size of small computers, the large, expensive mainframes gradually gave way to "server closets": racks of cheaper computers that could be more easily replaced and maintained.

As computing needs grew, some companies overflowed their server closets or server rooms and began dedicating entire buildings as "data centers." Remember what we said about mainframes requiring special cooling? That was even more true of the fiery hotness of data centers. Add in fire suppression systems, security guards, constant maintenance when hard drives failed or servers crashed, and you can understand how IT expenditures were going through the roof.

(You might be wondering why IT kept getting more expensive if individual computers were getting cheaper. This is an interesting dilemma called the Jevons paradox. It turns out that when we make something easier to access—electricity, hot water, streaming television, computers, whatever—people consume *more* of it. So costs go up, but ideally that's because we're getting much more value.)

Hosted Data Centers: Mainframes as a Service

Once enough people got a taste of running their own data centers, a lot of people got a taste for not doing that anymore ever again. And into the breach stepped a number of *managed hosting providers*. They'd run the data center for you. And instead of you buying servers and buildings to put them in (known as capital expenditures, or CapEx), you could just rent server time by the month (operational expenditures, or OpEx). For reasons that have never been fully clear to me, corporate accountants often prefer OpEx.

Somewhere along the line, the most advanced of these hosting providers, the ones with the best features and the most reliable services, became known as *cloud providers*. And today, you can rent compute time, storage space, or any number of higher-level managed services over the Internet with just a few clicks of your mouse. We've come full circle: just like you relied on a mainframe for central processing tasks in the 1970s, today much of your work may happen on cloud servers through web apps like Salesforce or Google Docs. Under the hood, complex automation is performing "timesharing" for you across thousands of cloud servers.

So is the cloud just a mainframe with extra steps? No, that's not really fair to say. A mainframe typically serves just one company or university. The cloud providers host software for millions of customers. Because of this, they're able to tune and refine their offerings to produce services that operate at higher and higher levels of abstraction. It's like having a great hive mind working on your behalf, solving problems before you even know you're going to have them.

It's getting to the point where the cloud is less of a product and more of a utility, like electricity or water. You can expect to turn the spigot and get IT on tap. If you ask me, that's a pretty highly evolved state of affairs.

Chapter 3

THE INTERNET: HOW CLOUD GETS LOUD

The Internet is the first thing that humanity has built that humanity doesn't understand.

—ERIC SCHMIDT

Unplug the router and plug it back in.

—YOUR DAD

The cloud has a problem. A big one, if we're fair:
If my computer is HERE, and my data is THERE,
Then how does it travel over all those miles of WHERE?

Let's break up that big problem. And here's how we'll attack it:
We'll divvy up our data, and we'll call each chunk a PACKET.

(These li'l guys are packets. It says so on their jackets.)

If your data is a movie, an installment of a show—
Then every packet has a tiny piece of video
And a destination address that instructs it where to go.

Now the rules that govern packets, from the big ones to the small,
Are the most important standard in the network world, that's all:
They're the VIP, the valuable INTERNET PROTOCOL.

And those addresses that guide our packets so they don't digress—
So they reach their destinations with unparalleled success—
You may have seen them. Each is known as one IP ADDRESS.

But addresses are not like maps.
They don't reveal the way.
There isn't one enormous wire
between points B and A.
The journey from the cloud to
you is twisted and outré.

(If what we're going to learn seems
inefficient, don't forget
The military scientists who built the
Internet
Decentralized the network to
withstand a Cold War threat.)

ROUTER · 1 HOP
ROUTER · 1 HOP
ROUTER · 1 HOP

The cloud computer has a map
(a ROUTE TABLE) to show
The closest network ROUTER
where the packets ought to go.
But does this end the journey?
In a lot of cases, no.

JOBS IN THE CLOUD: NETWORK ENGINEER

ROUTE TABLE

Those network packets don't just know
The places that they ought to go.
A human needs to help them steer:
An awesome NETWORK ENGINEER.

They calibrate the routing tables,
Giving them the proper labels,
Locking, blocking, making sure
That network traffic is secure.

In the cloud, their work is shifting;
Software does the heavy lifting,
Letting them administrate,
At which, no doubt, they're also great.

Should packets slow, should traffic stall,
You'll want these engineers on call
To poke about among the data,
Clear the jam, and see you later.

The router looks at ITS route table, ponders the abyss,
Forwards on the packet, and blows a little kiss.
(Routers, for the doubters, are emotional like this.)

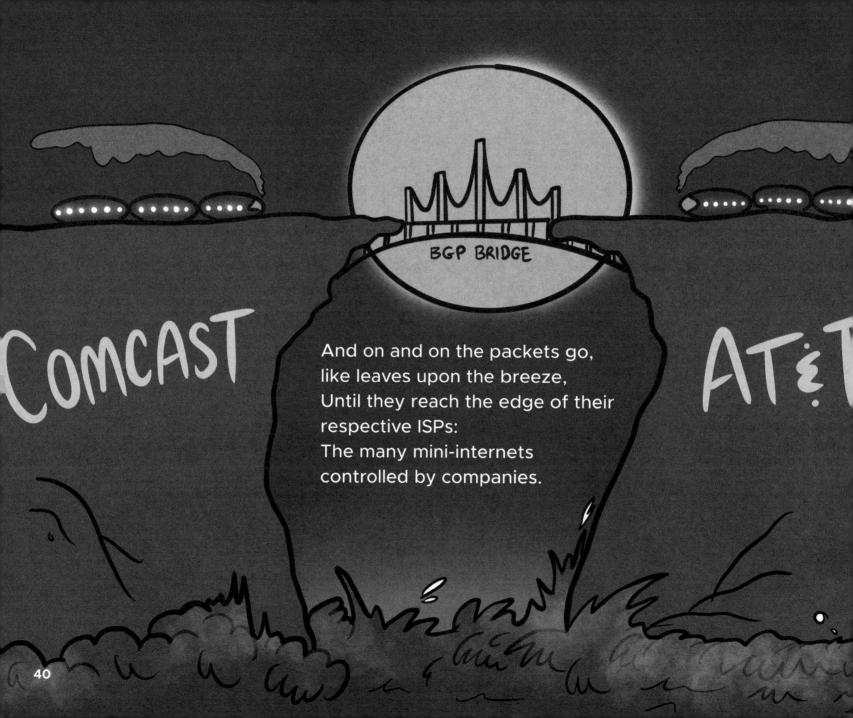

COMCAST

BGP BRIDGE

AT&T

And on and on the packets go,
like leaves upon the breeze,
Until they reach the edge of their
respective ISPs:
The many mini-internets
controlled by companies.

They stand upon the precipice, they rush out on the lines:
THE BACKBONE OF THE INTERNET, the fiber-optic spines
That run beneath the land and sea like massive buried vines.

Then hop again and hop again, from router unto route,
The packets travel one by one, until they tumble out
In your tablet with the content that your TV show's about.

43

twitter

fort

facebook

ins

amazon

snapchat

44

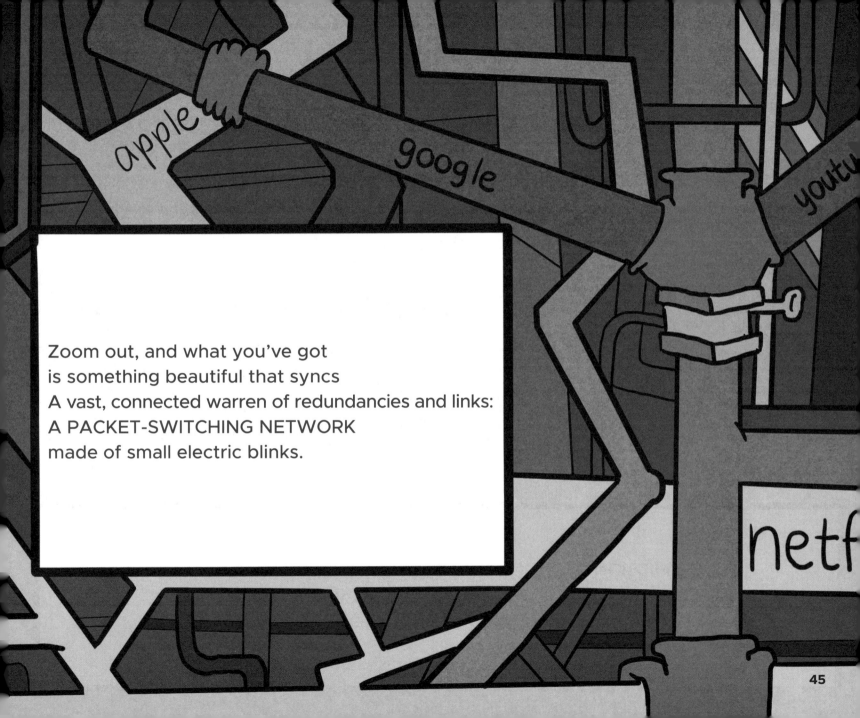

Zoom out, and what you've got
is something beautiful that syncs
A vast, connected warren of redundancies and links:
A PACKET-SWITCHING NETWORK
made of small electric blinks.

The Internet's not perfect, though. Neither is your PC.
The packets may not always reach their final addressee.
So we build other protocols to help out ol' IP.

TRANSMISSION CONTROL PROTOCOL, or TCP, is one.
It helps make sure the packets get transmitted till they're done.
And if they're out of order, it reshuffles them. That's fun.

TCP establishes the network connection using a HANDSHAKE of back-and-forth IP packets.	
TCP sends each packet of the message.	
When the recipient gets each packet, it returns a confirmation packet called an ACK (for acknowledgment).	
If the ACK does not come back, TCP sends the dropped packet again.	
Finally, TCP closes the connection.	

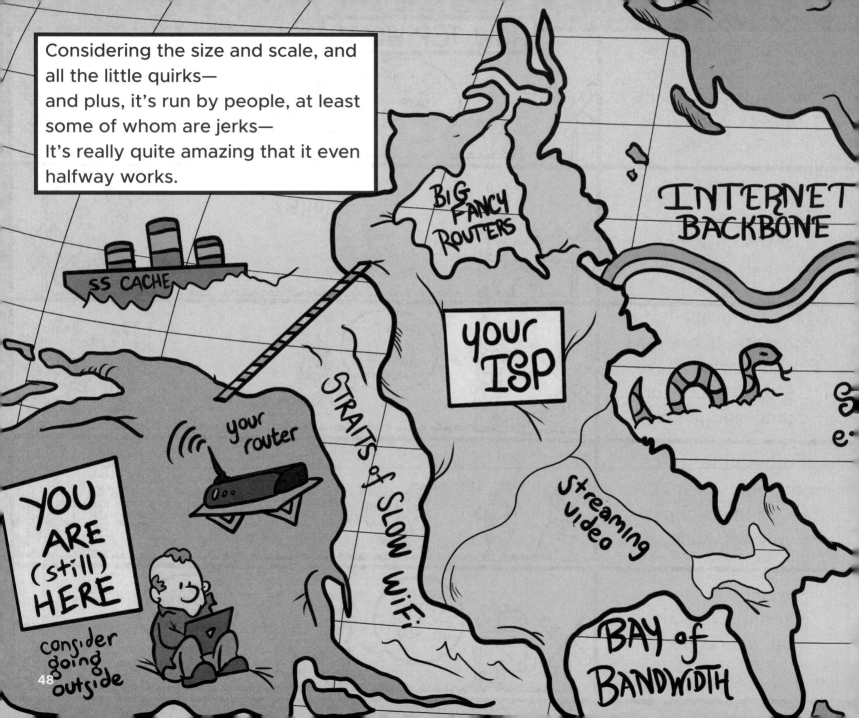

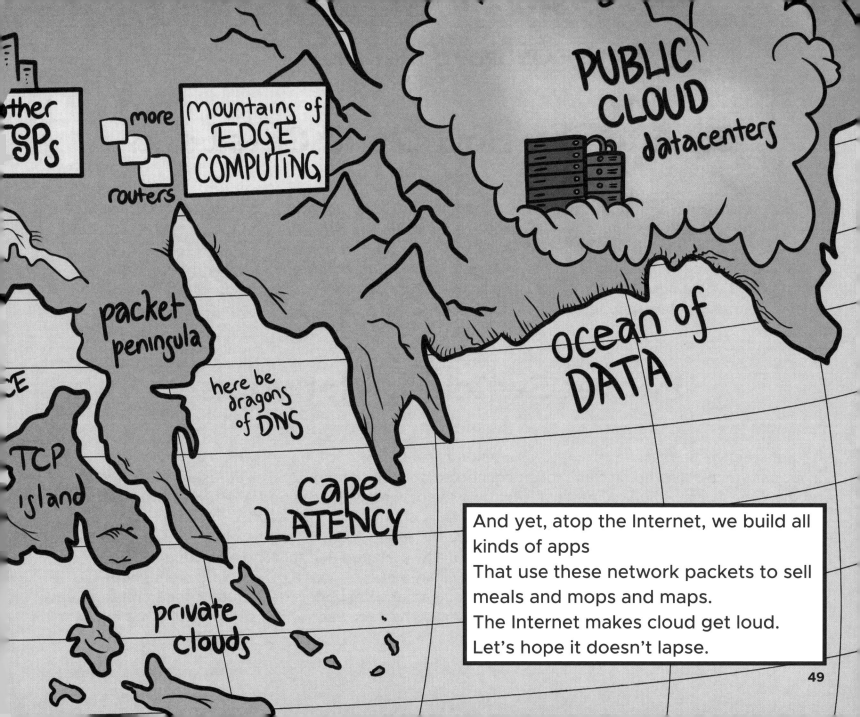

And yet, atop the Internet, we build all kinds of apps
That use these network packets to sell meals and mops and maps.
The Internet makes cloud get loud.
Let's hope it doesn't lapse.

49

The Internet: How Cloud Gets Loud

As Douglas Adams said about the universe, the Internet is big, really big; you won't believe just how vastly, hugely, mind-bogglingly big it is. On a typical Sunday, as I'm writing this, internetlivestats.com estimates that the world's 4.5 billion Internet users have fired off around five hundred million tweets, performed four billion Google searches, sent nearly two hundred billion emails, and moved an astounding five quintillion bytes of data (that's five billion billions!) across the countless cables that connect our computers, phones, televisions, and, well, pretty much everything.

Packet-Switching Networks

It's not strictly true that the Internet was intended as a communication network that could withstand a nuclear strike—in its first incarnation, it connected only four computers, all at research universities on the West Coast. (The first message sent over the new network, dubbed ARPANET, consisted of two letters: "LO." That sounds appropriately heraldic, though really researchers were trying to send the word "login" until the computer crashed.) But still, it was the 1960s, the Cold War was always a hot topic, and the early Internet engineers were military-funded and thinking existentially.

That's why the Internet doesn't have a central clearinghouse, like an old-fashioned telephone switchboard, that all traffic must pass through. Instead, the network is deliberately decentralized by using millions of specialized networking devices called *routers*, each with its own map (a *route table*) of places to forward traffic.

Internet traffic itself breaks down into tiny chunks of data called *packets*. Each packet can take a different route to its destination, sometimes traversing several different "hops" between routers along the way. If one router were to disappear, say because Khrushchev got frisky with some ICBMs, theoretically other parts of the network could continue communicating as the routers ping each other and figure out new traffic paths in real time. This is what we call a *packet-switching network*, and it has changed the world forever.

Internet Protocol

If you've been a citizen of the Internet for any length of time, you've probably encountered the notion of an *IP address*, which is the string of numbers and punctuation that identify your computer online.

IP stands for Internet Protocol, and it's more than just numbers. IP defines the structure of a data packet. IP addresses identify each packet and tell them where to go. All Internet routers and switches must understand IP to ensure that packets reach the correct destination.

Internet Protocol is that rare beast in the tech world: a universal standard. *Everything* speaks IP. Voice chat? That's voice-over-IP (VoIP). Remote desktops? PC-over-IP (PCoIP). Learn IP, and you have grasped the core of the Internet. The rest of the networking technologies fit around it like melee diamonds around the central jewel in a ring.

The Networking Stack

Most introductions to computer networking start by trying to explain something called the OSI model, which is a list of seven "layers" of networking, some of which are basically fantasy. Nobody worries about all seven of those layers in the real world. These are the important ones for you to know:

- **The physical layer:** The actual cables and switches that carry the electrical pulses of communication. If a shark bit through one of the undersea cables that make up the "backbone" of the Internet, which has happened, that would be a physical layer problem (as well as a shark intestinal problem).
- **The network layer:** IP. This takes care of how packets are packaged up and routed between network nodes.
- **The transport layer:** TCP (Transmission Control Protocol) and other higher-level protocols that govern how IP packets are sent and received. These protocols answer questions like, can I guarantee that the packets making up this message will arrive in order? If a packet dies in transit, will it get re-sent? If IP is the airplane, TCP is air traffic control.
- **The application layer:** The actual data payloads sent in the packets. This could be bits of streaming video, text for a web page, or anything you can express in ones and zeros. Lots of application-level protocols like HTTP govern the format of this data. But now we're past the realm of the Internet and into the domain of the software at each end.

BGP: How Networks Network

It would be wrong to think of the Internet as a single organism, like a brain, where every node is connected with equal weight. Rather, the Internet is balkanized, made up of many smaller networks that must figure out how to communicate with each other. Your Internet service provider (ISP)—like Comcast or AT&T—runs a mini-internet that forwards data to other ISPs to keep you online.

This process is far from straightforward and quite a bit beyond the scope of this book—it involves fiscal and political calculations, as well as constant vigilance over who to trust. (Imagine if I could convince your routers to send traffic into my evil network, pretending I was a valid destination!) Just know that there is some pretty interesting math called the Border Gateway Protocol involved, and it works way better than you would have any right to expect.

DNS

Finally, a quick word about the Domain Name System (DNS). DNS itself is a web service (some might even say a "cloud service") that translates the friendly names of websites, like wiley.com, into IP addresses so that your computer can communicate with the remote server to download the web page. If your computer hasn't talked to wiley.com before, it will have to contact the nearest DNS server. That server might need to talk to another server, and so on, up to a small number of authoritative *root name servers* around the world. The root name servers have the final word on what domain names map to which IP addresses.

If that sounds like a possible weak spot for the ol' nuclear apocalypse, well, you're not entirely wrong. Hackers frequently target root name servers with *distributed denial-of-service attacks* (see "The Great Cloud Heist (and How to Foil It)" in hopes of seriously damaging the Internet. Thankfully, though, the name servers are pretty resilient by now, and most computers cache the DNS names in case of a temporary outage, so it's probably okay.

The Internet Today

From massive undersea cables to the little modem in your closet, the Internet connects the modern world. It's brought along memes, trolls, Instagram, and a complete revolution of our lives and work.

We barely mentioned the word "cloud" in this chapter, and yet we didn't really have to. Without the Internet, the concept of cloud would be meaningless. You'd be back in the mainframe days, plugging your terminal into the central computer. The Internet puts more than just a world of information at your fingertips: it can turn any laptop into a supercomputer.

INTERLUDE: CLOUDSPOTTING

I am the daughter of Earth and Water,
And the nursling of the Sky;
I pass through the pores of the ocean and shores;
I change, but I cannot die.
For after the rain when with never a stain
The pavilion of Heaven is bare,
And the winds and sunbeams with their convex gleams
Build up the blue dome of air,
I silently laugh at my own cenotaph,
And out of the caverns of rain,
Like a child from the womb, like a ghost from the tomb,
I arise and unbuild it again.

—from "The Cloud," by PERCY BYSSHE SHELLEY

This looks pretty straightforward.

**—from "The Multicloud," by AN ENGINEER
WHO DID NOT KNOW WHAT HE WAS TALKING ABOUT**

There are so many kinds of clouds,
It's hard to spot them in the crowds.

The PUBLIC CLOUDS
are most well-known.
They're clouds that tech
behemoths own—
Like Microsoft or Amazon—
And you can build your apps upon.

Throughout this book,
when we say "cloud,"
We mostly mean the public crowd.

a public
cloud!

unpleasant

Now, PRIVATE CLOUDS
are public's foes.
They're data centers run by those
Who think the public cloud's a scam.
Insisting "I'll stay where I am!"
They're sure it's smart to stay
on-premises
But sometimes, they're their own
worst nemeses.

HYBRID CLOUDS are halfway creatures
Private, with some public features.
Run your servers in their rack;
Use the cloud for extra slack.
Hybrids often limp on by
For years, poor Frankensteins, or die.

hideous!

what even is this

If public cloud's your cup of cider,
But you don't trust one provider,
MULTICLOUD may sound like fun.
You build your apps so they can run
On any cloud:
they're CLOUD-AGNOSTIC.
This costs big bucks,
makes your boss sick.

Last but not least,
here's one more, kids:
Pluck cloud services like orchids,
Gathering the best-of-breed
That meets each app's specific need.
They call this POLYCLOUD,
or some such.
Time will tell if it gets done much.

well that
looks nice

Chapter 4
THE MAGIC OF CLOUD

Any sufficiently advanced technology is indistinguishable from magic.

—ARTHUR C. CLARKE

At least we're not in the data center anymore.

—HANK THE IT DIRECTOR, WHO HAS SEEN A THING OR TWO

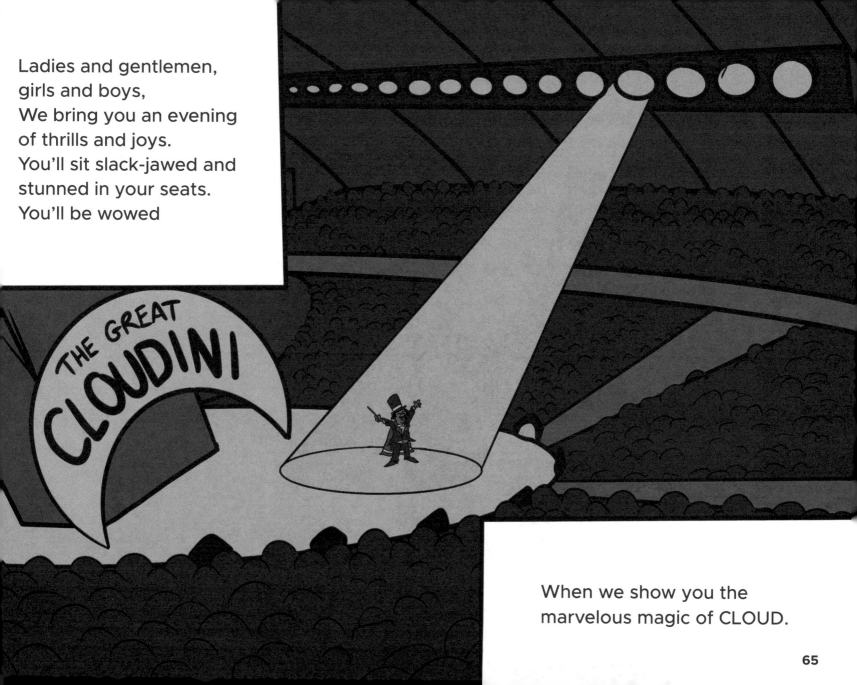

Ladies and gentlemen,
girls and boys,
We bring you an evening
of thrills and joys.
You'll sit slack-jawed and
stunned in your seats.
You'll be wowed

THE GREAT
CLOUDINI

When we show you the
marvelous magic of CLOUD.

Just look at this server
I hold in my hand.
It's small and unpowerful.
Frankly, it's bland.

When business gets busy,
these small servers fail.
But what if I told you...
this server could SCALE?

When traffic increases,
the cloud comes alive.
Where once we had
ONE server, now—
THREE, FOUR, FIVE!
The cloud has capacity
ready and warm
So our app stays online
in a SCALABLE form.

Now, watch very close.
Check my sleeves, check my gown.
When traffic DECREASES,
we auto-scale DOWN.

Not UNDERPROVISIONED, too tiny and cute,

Or OVERPROVISIONED, with too much compute—

From ten down to one, up to eight, back to three The cloud is ELASTIC. It's just right for me.

And plus, here's a doozy
of magical news:
I only get charged for
the servers I use!

I pay as I go,
whether lots or a little:
No contracts, no mess,
not a jot or a tittle.

TRICK OF THE TRADE: VIRTUALIZATION

When we show you "cloud servers," it's all sleight of hand.
VIRTUAL MACHINES, or "VMs," rule the land.
Special hardware per user would be kind of wasteful,
So the cloud uses software to keep scaling graceful.
On a physical server, like this one right here,
Hundreds of software VMs may appear—
Starting up, doing work, flashing out of existence—
Obeying the spells of our great cloud magicians.

Who keeps up these magical
servers, and where?
Hold on to your hats, folks:
you don't have to care!
The grunt work of managing
servers and storage
Is magicked away to
Nantucket or Norwich:
Some cool data center,
some smoothly run shop
While you just chill out,
building value on top.

The apps that you build, and the dollars you earn
Should hopefully dwarf any fees that you burn.
Not to mention—as cloud stuff gets better, a strange glow:
Your app improves all by itself! Presto change-o!

Then on top of the servers,
the cloud offers MORE:
More high-level services,
features galore.

Why build them
yourself when the
cloud has them cheap?
Just glue 'em together:
Small step, magic leap!

75

"But wait!" someone cries.
It's a terrified shout.
"Aren't you trapped in the
cloud with no way to get out?
"If you build on their services,
take what they give...
"When the cloud raises prices,
then how will you live?
"You can never escape back to
servers you own!
"Is this really a trick?
It's too horrid!" they groan.

Cloud lock-in, my friends, is no joke. Face your fear.
We must not understate: there is grave danger here.
To rely on a third-party vendor takes trust.
But to thrive in this cloud-native world, well...we must...

So stand on the shoulders of giants below you!
The cloud has a world of enchantment to show you.
It works like a charm, bringing wonder and laughter!

Except when it doesn't. But that's the next chapter.

78

A Scaling Horror Story

Ever seen a kangaroo do a facepalm? Me neither, but then I wasn't anywhere near the Australian Bureau of Statistics in 2016. These are the people who take the census for the entire country-slash-continent, and that year for the first time they decided to accept all the mandatory census forms online.

That meant having servers online ready to handle the traffic, and oh boy, did the Aussies think they were ready. They did capacity planning, which means they fired up a spreadsheet and figured out how many people they thought would be using the census app at any given moment; then they spent millions of dollars on servers to handle that load. Then they did load testing, which means they spent even more money throwing fake traffic at their servers to make sure everything looked good. Everything looked good.

But it wasn't good. It was, in fact, bad, and that became clear when the entire country of Australia got online to fill out their census forms at the same time and overwhelmed the system. The site crashed, a million #CensusFail memes swept the Internet, and the census bureau suffered something like $24 million in damages.

Autoscaling

The ABS failed because they couldn't *scale*: they didn't have enough server capacity to meet the demand of ten million Aussies and their clicky, clicky little computer mouses. And it turns out this is a big reason to use the cloud rather than your own data center, because scaling is kind of the cloud's thing. Not only does the cloud contain literally millions of servers, they also provide automation that makes it easy to autoscale them.

You can think of autoscaling like the suit Elastigirl wears in Pixar's *The Incredibles* movies. The suit stretches as far as she can, and the cloud can provide as many—or as few—servers as necessary to handle the user load your app is experiencing at any given moment.

That's really the central revolution of the cloud: having *exactly as many compute resources as you need, at any given time.* Back in the bad old days, you had to do capacity planning months or years in advance, purchasing hardware based on little better than a guess about how much you would need. So you always spent too much money up front by buying extra servers or ran the risk of an unexpected traffic increase taking you down like the Australian census bureau. (This also happened with regularity in the early days of Twitter—remember the "fail whale"?)

Pay-as-You-Go

The cool side effect of autoscaling is that you only have to pay for resources you actually consume. You don't have to sign contracts with cloud providers (although they'll often give you discounts if you do). You can just pay a monthly bill based on how much server time or storage space you used. Yes, this has an added marginal cost. But it gives a lot of flexibility to your business.

Having a bad month? Not many visitors to your website? Your overhead expenses for cloud will be lower. Going viral? You'll scale up and spend more—but ideally all that extra traffic translates into more business, so you're winning either way. The cloud brings powerful economic forces to bear on your behalf, linking your IT expenses directly to your business success.

No Maintenance

But the raw infrastructure cost of the cloud doesn't begin to capture the full value of using cloud services rather than running your own hardware.

After all, time costs money as well. Time to replace failed servers. Time to patch security flaws and automate infrastructure. Time to wake up at 3 a.m. because a bunch of overzealous Australians are setting fire to your census app. By automating many of the difficult and boring tasks of system administration, cloud lets you focus on the tasks that bring greatest value to your business.

Like writing the code for a better census. Two Australian college students saw the ABS fiasco and spent a weekend—48 hours!—building a cloud-native version of the app from scratch. Their little project handled *400 times the traffic* of the government's multimillion dollar boondoggle without turning a hair, delighting the media and further embarrassing the census bureau.

Continuous Improvement

Here's one more, often-overlooked benefit of cloud: cloud applications get better over time *without any effort on your part.* The cloud providers employ thousands of people whose job is to analyze the performance of their services at huge scale, develop new features, fix bugs, and release improvements. It's a common experience with cloud applications to wake up one day and discover that your servers are responding faster than yesterday or that your storage service has a new, cheaper tier.

This isn't just a nice thing; for people coming from the world of "on-premises" computing, it practically feels like a violation of the Second Law of Thermodynamics. We're used to systems that crumble and decay without constant drudgery on our part to keep them in working order. The cloud turns those expectations upside down.

(Side note: we talk a lot about "servers" in this book, but we don't necessarily mean physical computer devices. Not directly, anyway. Cloud providers use "virtualization" technology to run dozens or hundreds of virtual machines, or software programs that are pretending to be servers, on the same host. Since today's physical servers usually need just a fraction of their RAM and CPU to serve a single user's workload, multitasking with lots of VMs is a smart idea.)

The Lock-in Meme

Not everyone loves the cloud. And if those people were to read all the enthusiastic words I just wrote (though most of them aren't big readers), they'd smirk: "Yeah, but think about all the control you're giving up in the cloud. You're trusting the cloud provider not to go out of business, not to shut down a service you rely on, and most importantly not to raise prices on you. After all, when your whole business relies on them, what negotiating leverage do you have? The whole cloud thing is a trap to lock you in."

Vendor lock-in, usually through predatory contracts, is a story as old as IT. And while we haven't seen cloud providers ratchet up prices on consumers much as of this writing, it's not unreasonable to think it could happen someday. (Though I think, given how competitive the cloud space is, a wholesale price gouge would probably destroy the offending cloud along with its customers.)

But, as with every decision you make in life, you have to consider your risk. Realistically, how likely is your business to be hurt by an unprecedented cloud betrayal? And how likely is it to benefit from the autoscaling, value-based pricing, managed maintenance, and continuous improvement of cloud?

The Australian Bureau of Statistics has made their feelings clear on the subject. The next time they had to do a countrywide online survey, they built everything on cutting-edge cloud services. This time, there were no hiccups and no #CensusFail hashtags. And while you might never see a facepalming kangaroo, legends say that near the census office, the little critters are high-fiving to this day.

Chapter 5

RESILIENCE: HOW THE CLOUD STAYS UP

Only those who dare to fail greatly can ever achieve greatly.

— ROBERT F. KENNEDY

I blame the network.

—JANICE, A DATABASE ADMINISTRATOR

Look, even the cloud isn't perfectly flawless.
Computer equipment is scurvy and lawless.
The switches and drives in these glistening rows
May fail, and fail hard. And that's just how it goes.

BRAP
BRAP
BRAP

The software that runs the cloud might have a bug.

The janitor might slip and trip on a plug.

A shark might chow down on a key network link.

The point is,
the cloud's not as "up" as you think.

The cloud uses a model called "SHARED RESPONSIBILITY."
The cloud provider takes care of the physical facility
To the best of their ability.

CLOUD DATACENTER KEEP OUT

(Failures can be contagious, so please be advised:
The rhyme and meter as we proceed may break down or become significantly compromised.)

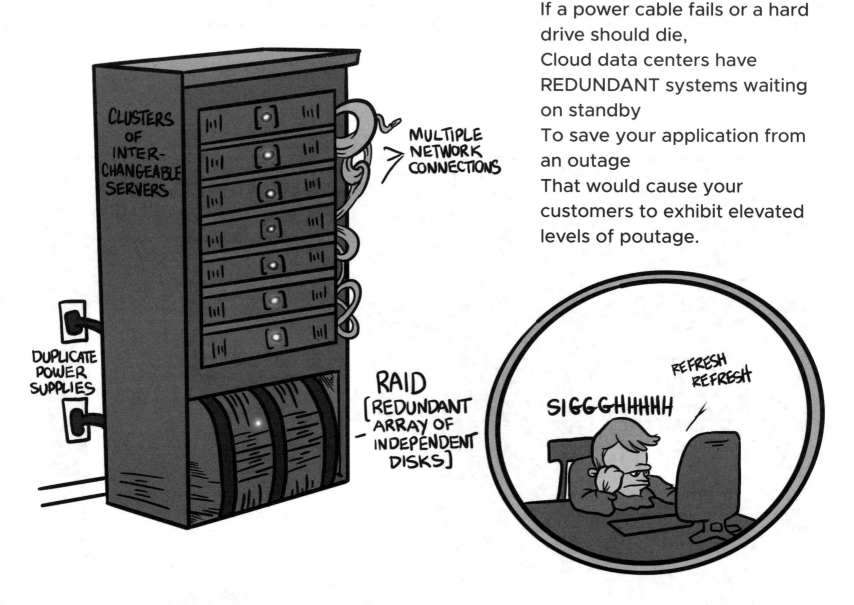

If a power cable fails or a hard drive should die,
Cloud data centers have REDUNDANT systems waiting on standby
To save your application from an outage
That would cause your customers to exhibit elevated levels of poutage.

CLUSTERS OF INTER-CHANGEABLE SERVERS

MULTIPLE NETWORK CONNECTIONS

DUPLICATE POWER SUPPLIES

RAID [REDUNDANT ARRAY OF INDEPENDENT DISKS]

SIGGGHHHHH

REFRESH REFRESH

JOBS IN THE CLOUD: CLOUD ENGINEER

He wakes at night. His pager beeps.
He sets aside his troubled sleep.
Another midnight job is here
To greet this great CLOUD ENGINEER.

He'll tell you that he works in "ops,"
A thankless task that never stops.
He won't reveal, unless you press,
He quite enjoys this blessed mess.

He does not trust his human hand
To build the clouds at his command.
His toolbox full of AUTOMATION
Runs the cloud in strict formation.

Sure, his work is plenty tough;
But that's why he enjoys this stuff.
The infrastructure he maintains
Upholds our digital domains.

They will also detect and replace failed hardware, whether underground or chest-high,
With efficiency and zest—aye,
It exceeds anything you could do if you had to go order the parts yourself from Best Buy.

THE CLOUD PROVIDER

YOU

Sometimes, not often — but often enough that you have to keep track, though — An entire data center is brought down by its natural enemy, the dreaded backhoe.

93

So clouds are built from multiple datacenters grouped close enough to minimize network latency, but far enough apart to avoid the possibility that they could get hit by the same runaway truckload of saxophones.

And these clusters of datacenters are called AVAILABILITY ZONES.

JOBS IN THE CLOUD: CLOUD ARCHITECT

When risk is high and clarity
Is lacking all across IT,
When other folks are circumspect,
We call on a CLOUD ARCHITECT.

As foreheads crease, as clouds
grow darker,
She picks up her whiteboard
marker
Illustrating, line by line,
The application's grand design.

Connecting storage with compute,
She renders watchers awestruck,
mute,
Revealing how the data flows
Between the services she chose.

Her work is an abstract affair—
She builds whole castles out of air.
Her powers of synthesis are freaky.
Even if her marker's squeaky.

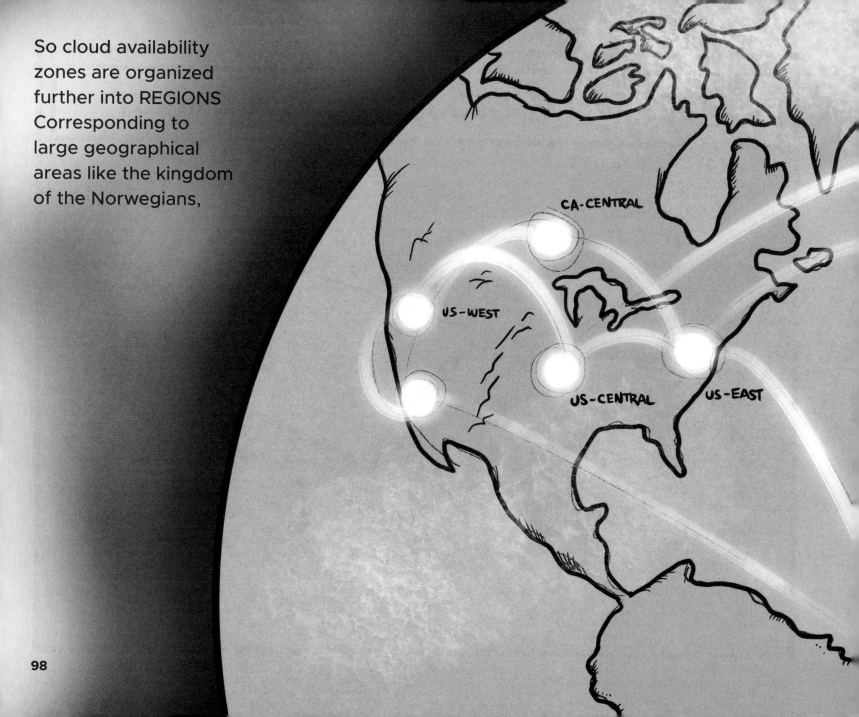

So cloud availability zones are organized further into REGIONS Corresponding to large geographical areas like the kingdom of the Norwegians,

98

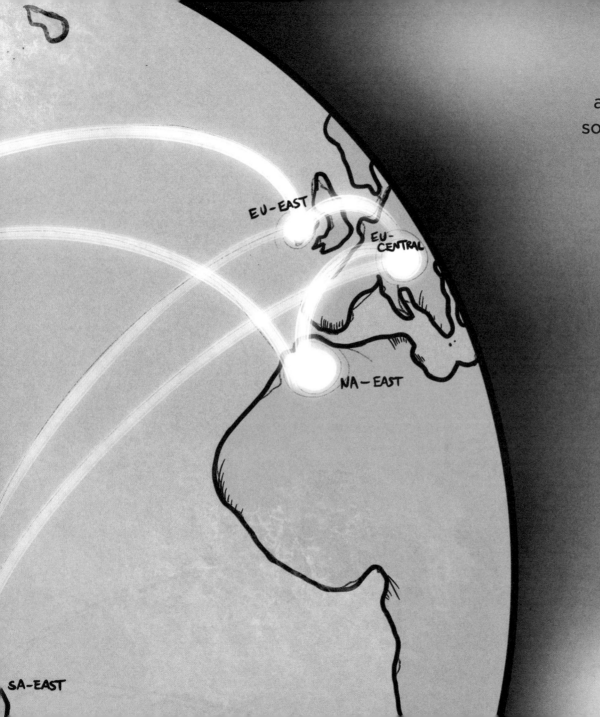

And should an entire region go down due to an earthquake or (worse) some radical dissolution of sociopolitical allegiance, You could just use another region, of which there are legions.

After all that, if your app falls over
and comes to a crashing halt,
I'm sure you'll agree with the cloud
provider that it's really your own fault
For not embracing the gestalt.

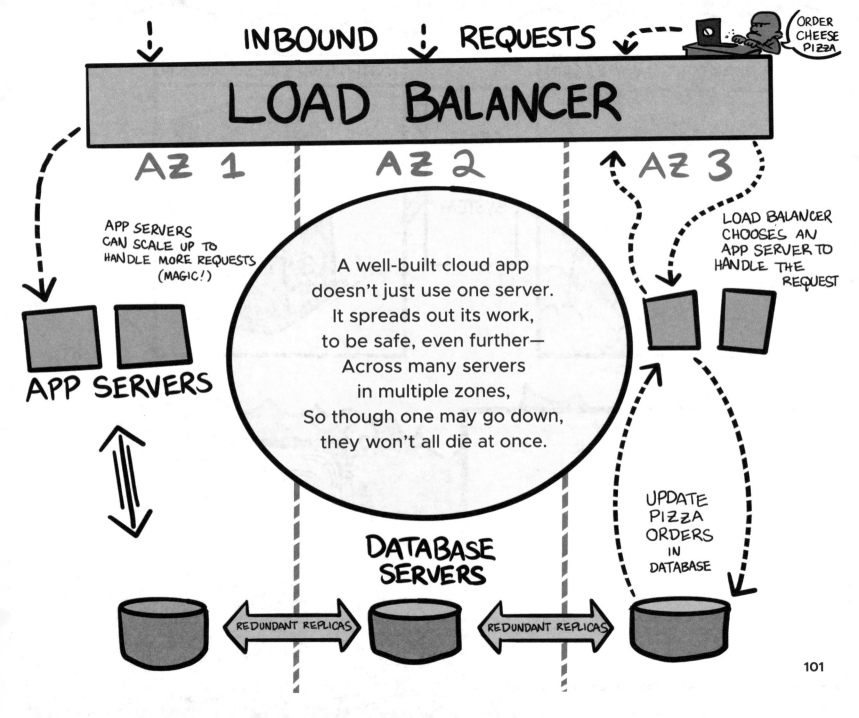

INBOUND REQUESTS

ORDER CHEESE PIZZA

LOAD BALANCER

AZ 1   AZ 2   AZ 3

APP SERVERS CAN SCALE UP TO HANDLE MORE REQUESTS (MAGIC!)

LOAD BALANCER CHOOSES AN APP SERVER TO HANDLE THE REQUEST

A well-built cloud app
doesn't just use one server.
It spreads out its work,
to be safe, even further—
Across many servers
in multiple zones,
So though one may go down,
they won't all die at once.

APP SERVERS

DATABASE SERVERS

UPDATE PIZZA ORDERS IN DATABASE

REDUNDANT REPLICAS   REDUNDANT REPLICAS

If a whole region dies,
then your app can "fail over"
And run in another,
like server Red Rover.
That kind of resilience,
mixed with agility,
Greatly sought after,
is HIGH AVAILABILITY.

If failover fails, to your great consternation, You're in a DISASTER RECOVERY situation, And you'd just better hope you have backups on hand To help with the careful restores that you planned. (You MUST test your backups. If not, you have sinned And your customers' data is lost in the wind.)

DATA BACKUP CELLAR

In closing—and this barely needs to be said—
The resiliency of the cloud is a massive improvement on
the old way of doing things, which sometimes amounted
to running your business from a server that you kept in a
pile of dust bunnies under your bed.

Resilience: How The Cloud Stays Up

The cloud's not perfect. It isn't supposed to be. In fact, we describe good cloud architectures not as "foolproof," but "fault-tolerant."

The Shared Responsibility Model

When you make the big decision to put your data on a cloud provider's servers instead of running your own hardware, you give up a certain amount of control—for better and worse. You are still responsible for the software of your cloud applications, like making sure your code doesn't have bugs in it. But the hardware—including the physical security of the data center—is now the responsibility of the cloud provider. You just have to trust that they know what they're doing.

The good news: cloud providers are among the best in the business at taking care of data centers and the machinery inside. After all, they do it at simply enormous scale. Amazon's S3 (Simple Storage Service) hosts data on the order of multiple exabytes—think a trillion copies of David Foster Wallace's *Infinite Jest*—and they run integrity checks on every single byte to maintain their legendary eleven nines of durability. That's 99.999999999 percent likelihood that your data will not get lost in a given year. You are several hundred times more likely to be struck by a meteor than to lose a file in S3.

Amazon Web Services and other cloud providers are able to sustain these guarantees because their data centers use specialized hardware and software, as well as highly trained technicians, to minimize the consequences of failure. They quickly replace bad drives, provide redundant (duplicate) power supplies and network cables, and probably don't make grilled cheese sandwiches on the toasty backs of the servers, which is what I would do.

Availability Zones and Regions

The natural enemy of the data center is the backhoe. Nothing can ruin a clever data backup strategy faster than a giant shovel slicing through the fiber-optic cable outside the building.

So the major cloud providers all have a concept of "availability zones," which are groups of one or more data centers that are physically far enough apart to avoid sharing some sort of localized catastrophe like a sliced network link but close enough together that data can travel back and forth without too much latency, or communication delay. (Remember, the cloud has to obey the laws of physics, just like all of us schmucks here on the ground.)

Availability zones themselves are grouped into geographical "regions," usually comprising two or more zones. If an entire region were to go offline, that would be a bad day. Like if a giant meteor hit the East Coast of the United States. Or, as happened to Amazon in 2017, if some system administrator typed 100 when they meant to type 10 and accidentally restarted too many servers, causing a cascading failure that took down S3 in the US-East region and what seemed like half the Internet with it.

Designing for Failure

You can't control what happens if the cloud provider screws up their end of the shared responsibility model. But you are completely in charge of your end: designing your application for failure.

You must assume, at the least, that any given availability zone could get pulled out from under you at any time. So a well-architected cloud application places resources in multiple availability zones and uses a routing device called a "load balancer" to send client requests to whatever servers happen to be online.

The database is the part of your application that's always the easiest thing to screw up in a failure scenario: data can get lost, or just as bad, you could end up with multiple copies of your data that disagree. So databases often have complex "failover" protocols that let you place replicas of your data in different availability zones, though only one of them is actively writing new data at a given time.

Lose a region? You might be in a *disaster recovery* situation and have to take some downtime, an unscheduled outage, while you bring up a new copy of your application from backups in another region. (You should definitely always have backups!)

So yeah, the cloud takes away some control. But it also gives you a ton of options for how you can protect yourself from failure, whether bugs in your code or sudden hardware suicide. There's even a whole discipline called *chaos engineering* that breaks parts of systems on purpose to see how resilient they are. The cloud lets you do that at very low cost so that when the big failure happens, you'll be ready.

Chapter 6

THE GREAT CLOUD HEIST (AND HOW TO FOIL IT)

A common mistake that people make when trying to design something completely fool-proof is to underestimate the ingenuity of complete fools.

—DOUGLAS ADAMS

Sorry for the weird DMs everybody, I think I was hacked!

—YOUR FACEBOOK FRIEND WHO SELLS ESSENTIAL OILS OUT OF HER GARAGE

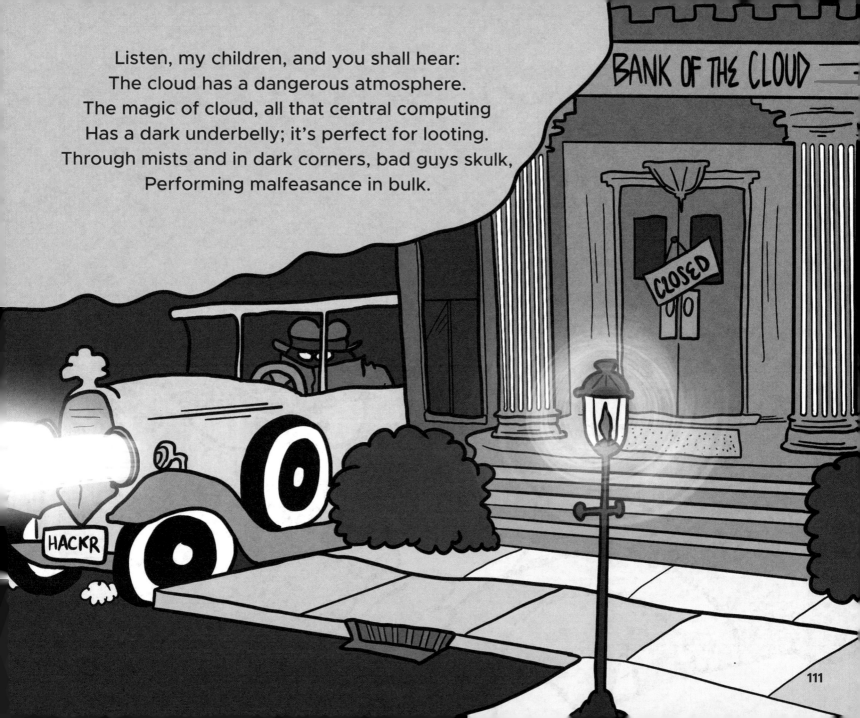

Listen, my children, and you shall hear:
The cloud has a dangerous atmosphere.
The magic of cloud, all that central computing
Has a dark underbelly; it's perfect for looting.
Through mists and in dark corners, bad guys skulk,
Performing malfeasance in bulk.

So much data, so much loot.
All in one place; ain't that cute?
Never seen servers so well-endowed.
So how do we hack the cloud?

HORSE ESCAPES,
THEN CLOUD LOCKS BARN
SORRY ABOUT THE IDENTITY THEFT
CREDIT MONI-TORING
CREDIT CARDS WORTHLESS
DARN, DARN, DARN

But what if we're burned by a strong firewall?
What if we can't get in at all?

A DDoS can work in mysterious ways.
Even if the cloud can handle the craze
All that dastardly data's expensive,
it is. Yes—
A "BILLING DDoS"
can put you out of business.

But this is all wrong.
These are not good cartoons.
Somebody's gotta
stand up to these goons!
How can the good guys
foil the hack?
How can the cloud
fight back?

JOBS IN THE CLOUD: SECURITY ENGINEER

When hackers prowl, when good guys flee,
It's time to call SECURITY.
The bad guys always leave a
trace.
This sharp-eyed
lawman's on the case.

He will protect; he must defend.
Opposing, to the bitter end,
The fiendish foes who haunt the cloud—
Though they assail him, he's unbowed.

He guards the cloud perimeter
And, acting as a limiter,
He stops attacks before they start.
He's gallant, sure, but also smart.

If (ghastly thought!) his watch should fail,
And cybercriminals prevail,
Then chaos would consume us all.
And so we're glad he's on that wall.

First, if you want to get rid of bad actors
Protect all your logins with two or more factors—
Not just a password, but also your phone.
Something you know, plus something you own.

Inevitably, when an endpoint gets breached,
Take measures to limit the bad guys' reach.
Encrypt all your data at rest and in transit.

Give servers and services just the permissions
They need. Limit access to rigid conditions.
You'll wall up your cloud in a thorn-covered hedge
With THE PRINCIPLE OF LEAST PRIVILEGE.

And if someone sneaks through?
From a hostile world power,
Does something nefarious
You'd better make sure there's

If a special ops guy
or a corporate spy
deep in your system?
no way that you've missed 'em.

Put monitors, booby traps, bells, and alerts
On all your cloud services. I know it hurts
To admit that you're vulnerable, but you are.
When you live in the clouds, then a storm's
never far.

There won't be a newspaper
headline the day
That you fend off a hacker. But hey,
that's okay.
Vigilance, friends, is its own reward.
At least you won't ever get bored.

THE GREAT CLOUD HEIST (AND HOW TO FOIL IT)

The cloud isn't *less* secure than, say, your personal hard drive. In many ways it's much more secure: it's professionally managed, probably uses good encryption by default, and is less likely to be accidentally dropped in your toilet.

However, because cloud systems centralize large amounts of data, the actions of a single hacker can be *devastating.* Like the 2013 Yahoo breach that exposed more than one billion user accounts, or Dropbox's 68-million-user barf that ended up with hackers selling the stolen accounts on the dark web for bitcoin. Leave a server online with an unprotected Internet port, or upload data to a data storage bucket without password protection, and you're pretty much asking to have your entire company held for ransom, as in the attack that destroyed the web hosting outfit CodeSpaces in 2014.

Even if the bad guys can't break into cloud systems, they can still take them down using an attack called a distributed denial of service (DDoS). They'll flood your servers with billions of junk network packets from all directions, overloading the application and forcing it offline. Cloud apps can actually be vulnerable to a unique flavor of this attack that I call a "billing DDoS": even if your servers can handle all the bogus traffic, the cloud's magical scaling powers could cause you to consume so many expensive cloud resources that the attack empties your wallet.

Hackers don't just target caches of data held by big companies, though. They'll also go after your personal accounts, like the guy who tricked multiple Hollywood celebrities into sharing their iCloud passwords with him back in 2012 (a process known as "phishing") and then stole their private photos from the backup service. In that case, the cloud system worked as designed. The problem was human error—well, celebrity error, but close enough.

Actually, that's par for the course. A recent Gartner study predicted that 99 percent of cloud security breaches over the next five years will be *the customer's fault.* It's that darn shared responsibility model again. The cloud providers are handing you power tools; it's up to you not to slice your hands off.

Preventing Data Breaches

The good news is that proper cloud security isn't some arcane mystery. As with most difficult things, like eating vegetables or working out, it's simple, good for you, and a little boring.

Use Proper Login Hygiene

Whether you're an individual or a professional system administrator, don't live and die by the strength of your password alone. Use multifactor authentication (MFA) to require something else on login, like a code from your phone or a scan of your fingertip. That way, even if the bad guys skim your password, they won't be able to do anything with it.

All the normal password advice applies too: use an unpredictable passphrase (not your dog's birthday or "Password123"); don't reuse passwords across sites (a password manager can help with that); and, of course, flip your passwords over four times a year. Or maybe that's mattresses. Oh well, it can't hurt.

It's also a good idea to enter your email address at haveibeenpwned. com and see if it's been exposed in any known breaches. (Don't worry, I didn't just send you to a phishing site, though at this point you're right to be suspicious!)

Encrypt Everything

There are two ways to encrypt cloud data: *at rest*, meaning while the data is being stored somewhere, like in a database, and *in transit*, meaning while the data is flying through the Internet in little packets. Encryption at rest is like putting money in a safe; encryption in transit is like putting it in a Brinks truck. Both are necessary to protect important data. (What data is important? You're on your own there, pal.)

Encryption algorithms are notoriously tricky to implement correctly, so we can all be thankful that many cloud services handle this out of the box these days. Make sure you are using SSL for your network communications (look for the "https://" at the front of secure links), and enable encryption on data stores if necessary, though at this point a lot of them do it by default.

Use the Principle of Least Privilege

Human users aren't the only entities with cloud logins. Software systems have them too. The cloud servers running your social media app or food delivery service have system credentials that let them talk to each other and share data as needed.

That's because cloud applications are often made up of *microservices*: little mini-systems that communicate with each other over the network. Each microservice is supposed to do a separate, unique piece of work, like sending emails or generating reports. The thing that sends you a text message when your hair salon is running a special is probably a microservice.

From a security standpoint, the challenge with microservices is making sure they only have access to do the things they are supposed to do. It's much easier for cloud developers to leave system credentials unrestricted, avoiding the possibility of an error when a request between services gets denied. But, of course, when you leave permissions open too wide, you increase the risk that a hacker who compromises *one* microservice can jump to *others*, causing very macro amounts of damage.

I think I learned in school that the *Titanic* sank because the watertight compartments in the hold were supposed to be individually sealed, but when the iceberg hit, water spilled from one compartment to the next until the whole ship went down. You don't want your app to be the next *Titanic*, so obey the *principle of least privilege*: give applications and services (as well as users) only the rights they need to accomplish their specific task. By layering these permissions, you create *defense in depth*: a strategy minimizing the chances of exposure, like wearing three pairs of socks with holes in different places.

Detect as Well as Protect

In 2015, hackers broke into the U.S. Office of Personnel Management's databases and stole more than 4.2 million personnel files of current and former government employees. The breach targeted the sensitive information that workers submit for security clearance, not just Social Security numbers but also the names and addresses of family, interviews with college friends, and mental health history. The kind of soul-baring confessions that could be used to blackmail key government figures. So, yeah, important data.

But here's the worst part: the leaks went on for *more than a year* before Office of Personnel Management (OPM) noticed. They only figured it out when a third-party contractor accidentally stumbled on the breach during a sales demo of a forensic tool, which must have been either the greatest or worst demo in the history of mankind.

Oh, and the method of the hack? It wasn't some evil genius laying waste to a network firewall. The attackers just phished an employee's password. At the time, the OPM did not require multifactor authentication.

Moral of the story: Check for abnormal access patterns in your system, like sessions from unusual IP addresses. Automate those checks if possible. And, of course, require MFA! The alternative is a hack that destroys your business, or at least leads to costly and embarrassing mitigations.

I should know; I was an OPM hack victim myself. The government is still paying to send me credit monitoring notices.

Chapter 7

THE TELLTALE TOILET: AN IoT HORROR STORY

Privacy is not something that I'm merely entitled to, it's an absolute prerequisite.

—MARLON BRANDO

I swear that my phone is listening to me.

—YOUR NEIGHBOR MARGE

Once upon a midnight dreary,
while I watched *The Big Bang
Theory*,
On a giant smart TV I didn't have
the budget for—
While I watched my smart TV,
my smart TV was watching me.
Oblivious to my privacy, it
tracked my every blink and
snore.
Sending my behavior to
the cloud, which tracks me
evermore.

(Hey, computer, what's the
score?)

Cloud-enabled "smart" devices understandably entice us.
Hat racks, ice packs, toasters, coasters—all online, all streaming more.
But this "Internet of Things," along with all the fun it brings,
Comes with certain dangling strings: your privacy goes out the door.
Do I have control of all the data my devices store?
Quoth the trash can: "Nevermore."

BIG DATA
DATA LAKE

TVs track your home location. Smart lights know when you vacation.
All these gadgets stream your data to the cloud, where it will pour
Ceaselessly, by means opaque, into a central "data lake":
A massive, aggregate intake with insights washing on its shore.
This is what we call BIG DATA: What, pray tell, is it used for?
Quoth the smartwatch: "Wouldn't you like to know."

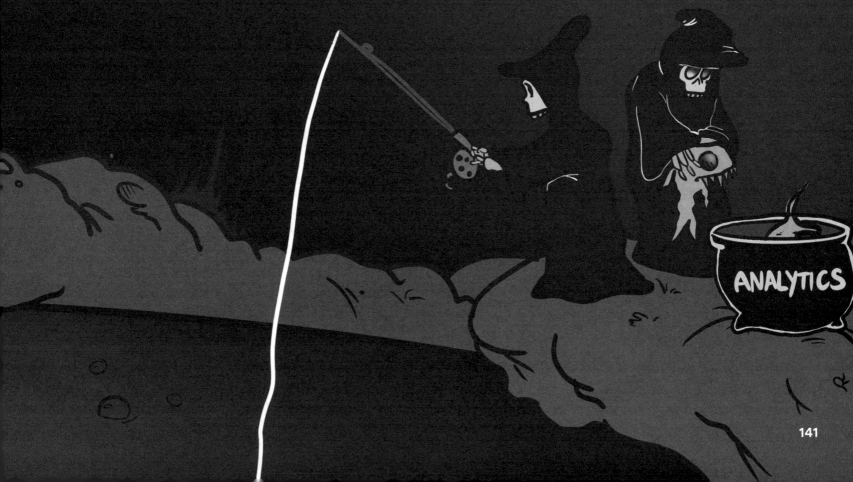

Has your friendly smart assistant ever broken faith and listened
Covertly, when you complained in privacy, behind closed door
Of your fiery pain when wiping? Did it sell your secret griping
To a sneering, stereotyping advertising megacorps?
Is that why you see these ads for creams and lotions more and more?

Quoth the toilet: "Your privacy is very important to us."

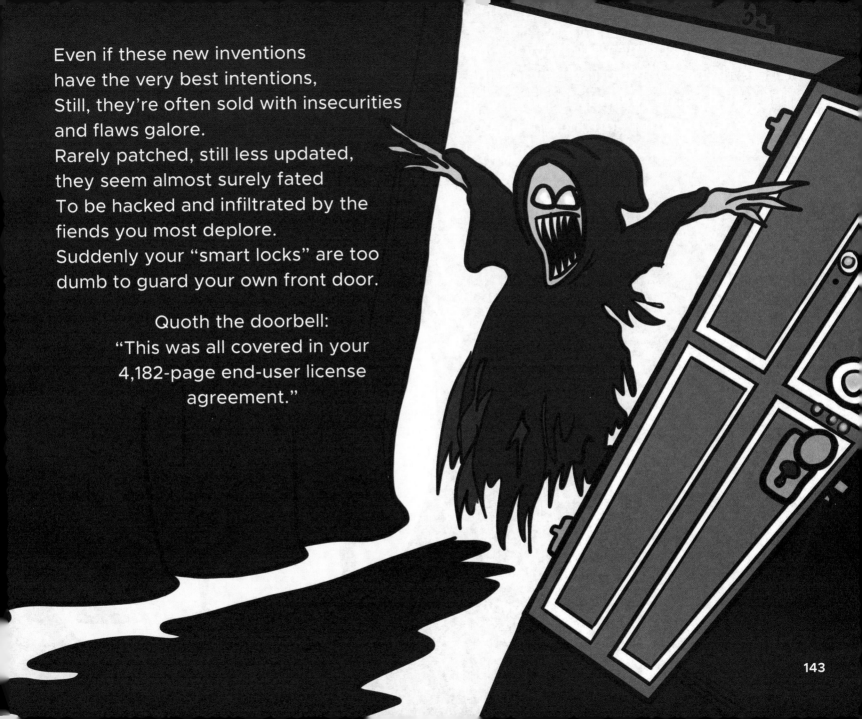

Even if these new inventions
have the very best intentions,
Still, they're often sold with insecurities
and flaws galore.
Rarely patched, still less updated,
they seem almost surely fated
To be hacked and infiltrated by the
fiends you most deplore.
Suddenly your "smart locks" are too
dumb to guard your own front door.

Quoth the doorbell:
"This was all covered in your
4,182-page end-user license
agreement."

Ask yourself, next time you fly by ice trays with embedded WiFi,
What are these contributing beyond the plain old ice of yore?
Do they give some real advancement, some specific life enhancement?
Are they maybe brief entrancement, nothing less and nothing more?
If the ice-cloud leaked that data, might the consequence be poor?

Quoth the smart speaker: "I'm sorry,
    I don't know that one."

THE TELLTALE TOILET: AN IoT HORROR STORY

"I'm your best friend," said the man's voice in eight-year-old Alyssa LeMay's bedroom. "I'm Santa Claus." Then the song "Tiptoe through the Tulips" began playing through the Ring security camera that her parents had installed above her dresser.

It had surely never occurred to Alyssa—before she ran screaming for her parents that night in December 2019—that a stranger might be spying on her through her nanny cam. But Mr. and Mrs. LeMay thought they had taken precautions: strong passwords, a secure network. The one protection they didn't set up—two-factor authentication—might be the reason their daughter refuses to sleep in her bedroom now. But there's really no way to know.

Stranger (Internet of) Things

"Internet of Things" might be the stupidest name in technology, but it's a pretty simple concept: stuff that didn't use to have an Internet connection but does now. Many industrial machines send data to the cloud as part of normal operation these days. But most of us are more familiar with IoT on the consumer side—smart TVs, smart fridges, even smart socks and toothbrushes. If you are wearing a smartwatch, you yourself are a thing on the Internet of Things.

But should you be?

So far, a lot of the stuff we've discussed in this book has been pretty abstract: virtual machines, availability zones. IoT is more fraught because a malfunctioning IoT device can have immediate and disturbing consequences in the physical world.

Security Concerns

In 2015, security researchers remotely stopped a Jeep on a St. Louis highway by hacking in through the car's entertainment system. A few years earlier, a disgruntled former used-car-lot employee had shut down hundreds of cars in Texas via an insecure vehicle-immobilization system.

The point is that when life and death are on the line, you'd better hope that your online devices are secure. And a lot of IoT devices aren't. Gadget companies are mostly incentivized to sell new, shiny toys—not to close security loopholes, and certainly not to keep up with security updates on older versions of their products. Researchers from Stanford University recently found that two-thirds of American households have at least one smart device, and millions of these devices are vulnerable to simple hacks over the Internet.

And if you're thinking, "Well, a hacker can't do much harm by compromising my Keurig machine," remember that these devices are usually on the same home WiFi network as your cameras, phone, and computer. Once the hackers get in, they've got all sorts of fun targets to explore.

Not every Thing has a bad security pedigree, though, so do your research before you buy—and even then, you may not have a full picture of what you're letting yourself in for.

Privacy Violations

If cloud security is about protecting your data from bad guys, privacy is about controlling what data you hand over to the cloud in the first place. Unfortunately, IoT takes a lot of that control out of your hands.

Most of the big tech companies make their money by selling your data to advertisers. So it's in their interest to collect as much information about you as possible—what we call "big data." And most of us have no idea how much is possible.

Smart TVs are such a bad offender in this category that the FBI has started posting warnings about them. These days, your fancy 75-inch monitor likely comes with a hidden but equally fancy camera and microphone: performing facial recognition to figure out what you've been watching, whether you like it, and maybe even what you're eating in front of the TV. This might not bother you. But if it does, there's not really any way to disable the tracking, or even complain.

Ever seen an ad for sunscreen right after talking to someone about your beach vacation? You're not crazy or paranoid—your smartphone really is listening to you and sends keywords back to the cloud for marketing purposes. (If you don't like this, turning off voice assistants might help—they're basically just always-on microphones in your pocket.)

Can IoT devices actually improve your life and by extension society? Sure. Smart thermostats are pretty cool (pun intended). Wearable devices that can detect medical emergencies, such as falls, have huge potential to help the elderly. Heck, Alexa has been subpoenaed as a murder witness. But simply because of the amount of data they collect and their direct influence on physical reality, IoT technologies must clear a high bar for safety and responsibility. (If everyone has a smart button that can automatically dial 911, how many bogus 911 calls will there be?)

Right now, little oversight of IoT devices exists—at least in the United States. And until something changes there, it's probably a good idea to assume that any smart speaker or camera in your house might have a stranger spying through the other end. That's why Alyssa LeMay's parents eventually got rid of the webcam in her bedroom. They, like so many other smart buyers, have learned to beware.

Chapter 8

GETTING YOUR HANDS CLOUDY

The cloud services companies of all sizes...
The cloud is for everyone. The cloud is a democracy.

—MARC BENIOFF

Explain it to me one more time.

—YOUR MOM, WHO REALLY WANTS TO UNDERSTAND

What is the cloud?
Is it friend or foe?
After reading this book,
Do you think you know?

It's a bit esoteric, it's somewhat abstract,
But I hope we've seized on a salient fact:
The next generation of builders and makers,
The bit farmers tilling the Internet acres—
The reason these fields of endeavor get plowed
Is the law of abstraction, the power of cloud.

CLOUD SERVICES

STARTUPS

FINANCE

GOVERNMENT

HEALTHCARE

EDUCATION

MANUFACTURING

No longer need entrepreneurs figure out
How to buy their own servers and tote them about;
You can purchase a service and pay as you go!
If that isn't power, then what is, I dunno.

Abstraction kills friction, which speeds innovation.
And that means impressive DEMOCRATIZATION
Of software delivery: anyone can!
You can build the next Uber in back of your van.

You can build a ReFloofer, a Fizz-a-ma-tazz.
You can make your own app teaching dogs to play jazz.

When you pay as you go, then you're limited by
Not the naysayers, friend, or the cloud, but the sky.

JOBS IN THE CLOUD: CLOUD DEVELOPER

If you like to build with bricks
That snap in place with pleasant clicks,
Then you are not so different from
A CLOUD DEVELOPER. How come?

Each cloud service is like a toy
That cloud developers enjoy.
They stack them higher, one by one.
Abstraction makes them laugh; it's fun!

While in between, they spread new code
Like glue, like mortar, load by load,
To mold a shape that's quite unique.
They test; they twist; they tease; they tweak.

And, with the edifice complete,
They've rendered something new and neat:
An app for all the world to play with.
That's the thing they have a way with.

UNPLANNED COSTS

But the cloud is potentially also a threat
To your privacy, safety, and technical debt.
Reflection and planning must all be allowed first,
Or else you might get yourself drenched in a cloudburst.

You may ask: What's next?
Is the cloud all there is
When it comes to deploying an Internet biz?

When learning technology, one
rule of thumb:
It's wise to predict more
abstraction to come.
The servers that made up the
cloud 1.0
Are starting to phase out,
they're starting to go
By the wayside in favor of
SERVERLESS services
Building cloud higher, for more
advanced purposes.
(Yes, there are still servers
somewhere down there.
But you don't have to know that.
You don't have to care.)

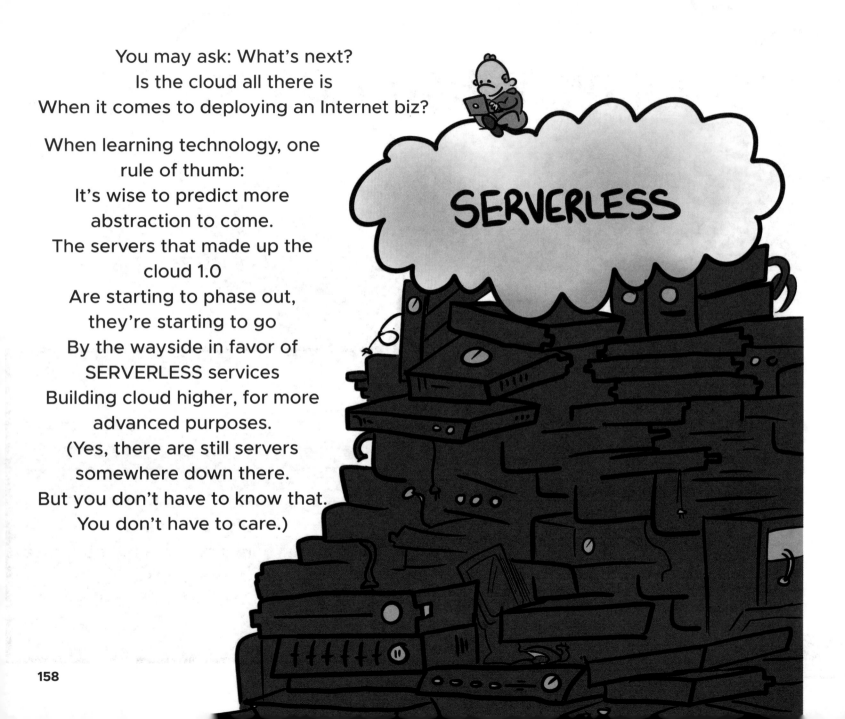

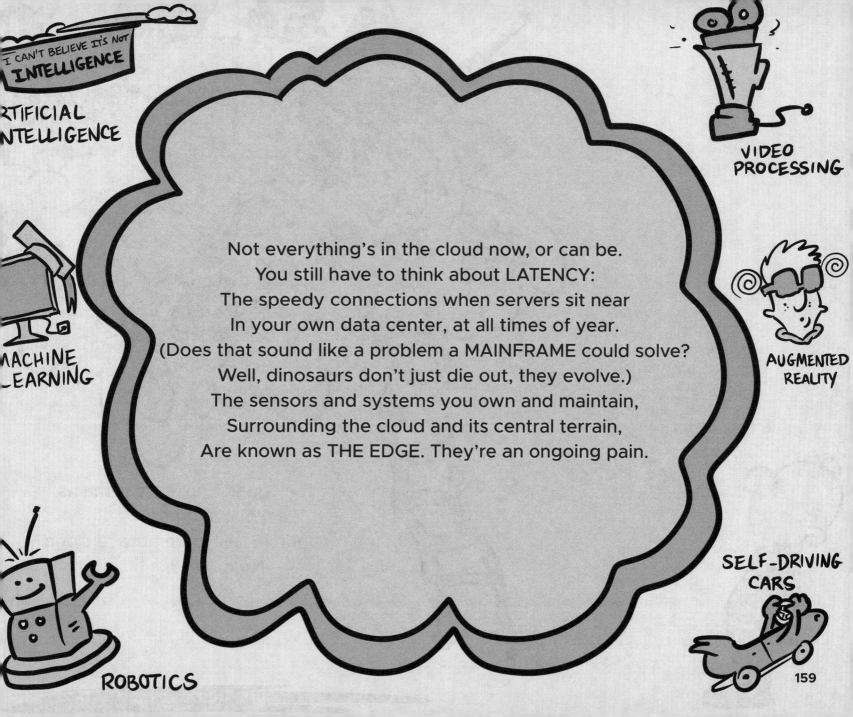

ARTIFICIAL INTELLIGENCE

I CAN'T BELIEVE IT'S NOT INTELLIGENCE

VIDEO PROCESSING

MACHINE LEARNING

AUGMENTED REALITY

Not everything's in the cloud now, or can be.
You still have to think about LATENCY:
The speedy connections when servers sit near
In your own data center, at all times of year.
(Does that sound like a problem a MAINFRAME could solve?
Well, dinosaurs don't just die out, they evolve.)
The sensors and systems you own and maintain,
Surrounding the cloud and its central terrain,
Are known as THE EDGE. They're an ongoing pain.

ROBOTICS

SELF-DRIVING CARS

159

Where it all goes from here remains
anyone's guess.
In the meantime, will you embrace cloud?
No or yes?

GETTING YOUR HANDS CLOUDY

If you take one thing away from this book, it should be that I'm very bad at drawing fish and trains.

But if you have a second takeaway, I hope it's that the cloud isn't just some inscrutable thing for you to passively consume.

The cloud is meant for you to build on. Yes, you.

Democratizing Computing

There's a reason essentially every startup company for the last few years—no matter the field—has built its IT infrastructure in the cloud, often disrupting competitors with decades of established advantage. Many reasons, in fact.

We've covered most of the reasons in one chapter or another, but let's recap them:

- Pay-as-you-go pricing lets people without a lot of money have access to world-class software services. If they build something successful that gets a lot of traffic, then the costs increase in parallel with their ability to pay.
- Cloud services *abstract away* basic IT tasks, so most people don't have to worry about them anymore. Werner Vogels, the CTO of Amazon, calls this kind of work "undifferentiated heavy lifting." That's a fancy way of saying hard work that doesn't need to be duplicated by every single company. Once Amazon or Microsoft gets a particular kind of database service right, there's no reason for every mom-and-pop company to build their own (worse) version. They

can just use the cloud provider's. That helps the little company spend less time on grunt work and more time building the unique, special thing that's their reason to exist. Like Netflix's movie library or Lyft's ridesharing algorithm—just to name two startups that grew at hyperspeed through aggressive use of the cloud.

- The cloud lets you collaborate from anywhere. Some of today's hottest tech companies are "fully remote": they have no physical office, and everyone works from home and communicates over cloud services like the videoconferencing tool Zoom and the chat app Slack. That lets you hire the best talent wherever they live, not relying on the local want ads. It also insulates you from unexpected problems in the physical world. It's safe to say that without the option of cloud communications, the world would not have been able to impose such drastic quarantine measures during the 2020 coronavirus pandemic.

These reasons, and more, have helped cloud adoption explode over the past decade. As 2020 dawned, 91 percent of companies were building at least some portion of their software in the public cloud, spending more than $400 billion to do it. And there is plenty of innovation still to come.

Serverless

As cloud providers continue to refine their offerings, they're selling more high-level services that are simple and easy to use. You might not know what to do with a virtual machine, no matter how easy it is to rent. But you probably can think of a use for Amazon's Polly service, which turns written text into speech—an automated way to create audiobooks and phone greetings. These days, you can stitch an entire software application together using mostly cloud services and writing very little new code.

"Serverless," a movement that has gained much prominence (and a bit of controversy) in the cloud engineering community over the past few years, tries to use cloud services whenever possible, writing new code only when absolutely necessary. Despite what the name implies, a serverless software application still runs on servers. (I'm not aware that there's any other way to run code!) But from the developer's perspective, the underlying servers are irrelevant: all they see is the cloud interface, so for them the experience appears seamless...and serverless. Whether the name catches on or not, the principles of cloud-first engineering developed by the serverless community are sure to play a big role in the next decade.

That's because analysts believe that the world will have jobs for 100 million software developers by 2030—and they will need simple tools that let them build quickly. Imagine writing code by giving conversational instructions to a virtual assistant ("Alexa, make me an inventory database"), which sends commands to a "serverless" software system in the cloud, which runs on virtual machines automated on physical servers mounted in three redundant data centers spread halfway across the country, each with their own security staff, maintenance crews, and disaster recovery protections. That's the future of abstraction, and it's closer than you think.

The Edge

Will all software eventually run in the cloud? Certainly not. Packets can only travel through the cables of the Internet at the speed of light, and so when you are talking to a cloud server halfway around the world, you'll experience some amount of lag time, known as *latency*. So some applications will always need to run on hardware that is physically close to the end user, not connected over the Internet. For example, algorithmic stockbrokers rely on nanoseconds of advantage to be first with a big trade, so they put their servers right in the same data center as the stock exchange—in the very next server rack if possible. (This is called *colocation*.)

Many industrial machines do not have reliable Internet connectivity, or they produce too much data to send it all to the cloud cost-effectively. These machines often process some of their data locally, right on the factory floor, before sending some or all of it to the cloud. We increasingly refer to local IoT devices that send some of their data to the cloud as *edge computing*. Edge devices are notoriously difficult to keep track of and keep updated, for reasons we've covered in the IoT chapter. But they're not going anywhere, so we just have to learn how to deal with them.

The Cloud and You

Even if you don't want to start a business, you're still living in the cloud—whether you like it or not, you don't have much choice at this point. It's up to you to be a responsible citizen.

- **Maintain your privacy:** Stay aware of services that collect your data without your consent.
- **Stay vigilant over security:** Use strong passwords and multifactor authentication.
- **Keep backups of your data:** You never know when lightning will strike.

And maybe, once in a while, step back to appreciate this thing that exists at the intersection of the Internet and our imaginations. This great big, magical, dangerous, colorful thing called the cloud.

Happy building,
Forrest

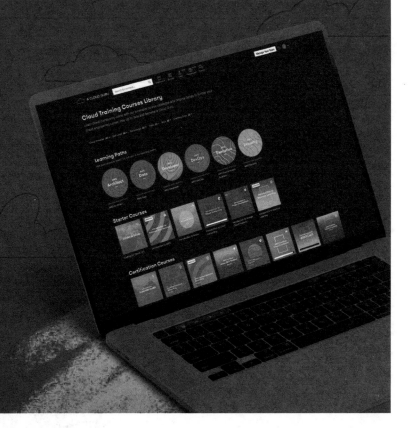